Machines at Work

Dump Trucks

by Rebecca Stromstad Glaser

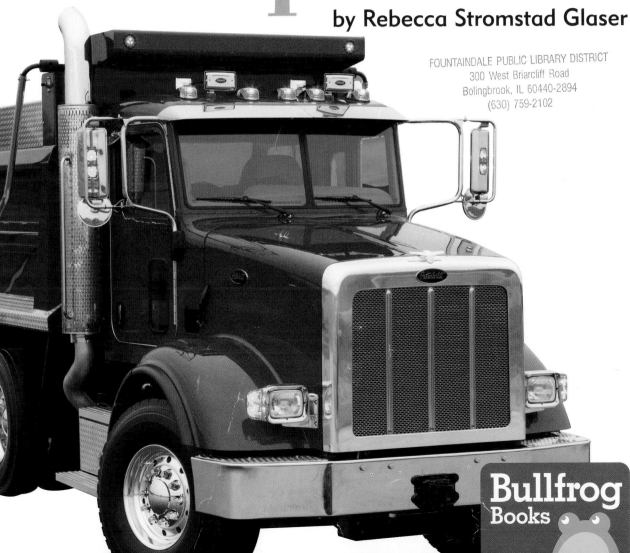

Bullfrog
Books

Ideas for Parents and Teachers

Bullfrog Books let children practice reading informational text at the earliest reading levels. Repetition, familiar words, and photo labels support early readers.

Before Reading:

- Discuss the cover photo. What does it tell them?

- Look at the picture glossary together. Read and discuss the words.

Read the Book

- "Walk" through the book and look at the photos. Let the child ask questions. Point out the photo labels.

- Read the book to the child, or have him or her read independently.

After Reading

- Prompt the child to think more. Ask: Have you ever seen a dump truck? What was it hauling?

Bullfrog Books are published by Jump!
5357 Penn Avenue South
Minneapolis, MN 55419
www.jumplibrary.com

Library of Congress Cataloging-in-Publication Data
Glaser, Rebecca Stromstad.
Dump trucks / by Rebecca Stromstad Glaser.
  p. cm. — (Machines at work) (Bullfrog books)
  Summary: "This photo-illustrated book for early readers describes the parts of a dump truck, different types of dump trucks, and the jobs they do. Includes photo glossary"
—Provided by publisher.
Includes bibliographical references and index.
Audience: Grades K-3.
ISBN 978-1-62031-019-9 (hbk.)
1. Dump trucks--Juvenile literature. I. Title.
TL230.15.G56 2013
629.224—dc23

2012008573

Series Editor: Rebecca Glaser
Series Designer: Ellen Huber
Photo Researcher: Heather Dreisbach

Photo Credits
Alamy, 5, 23tr; Dreamstime.com, 16–17, 23br; Getty Images, 16; iStockphoto, cover, 10–11; Peterbilt, 1; Shutterstock, 3l, 3r, 4, 6–7, 8–9, 12–13, 14, 15, 19, 20, 21, 22, 23bl; SuperStock, 18–19, 23tl

Printed in the United States of America at Corporate Graphics, North Mankato, Minnesota.
7-2012 / PO 1122
10 9 8 7 6 5 4 3 2 1

Table of Contents

Dump Trucks at Work

How can you move a big pile?

Call a dump truck!

A loader
scoops up dirt.
It fills the bed.

A driver sits in the cab.
She pulls a lever.

Ready to dump!

A ram lifts the bed.
It tips.

ram

The tailgate opens.
Swoosh! Dirt slides out.

tailgate

The bed
goes down.

Where is the
next job?

An old house is
smashed to pieces.

A dump truck
comes.

It takes the
pieces away.

13

A new house is built.

A dump truck brings gravel.
It is for a driveway.

An old road is chopped up.

A side dump comes.

It takes away the old pieces.

A new road is built.
A dump truck comes.
It lays long rows
of blacktop.

Where do you see dump trucks?

Parts of a Dump Truck

bed
The long open part of a truck where things are carried.

ram
A long pole that extends and lifts up a dump truck bed.

cab
The part of a truck where a driver sits.

tailgate
A gate at the back of a truck bed that lifts for unloading.

Picture Glossary

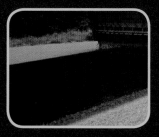

blacktop
A smooth, hard surface that covers roads.

loader
A machine with a big bucket on the front, used to put materials in a dump truck.

gravel
Small, loose stones used for roads and driveways.

side dump
A long dump truck that tips to the side instead of at the end.

Index

To Learn More

Learning more is as easy as 1, 2, 3.

1) Go to www.factsurfer.com

2) Enter "dump truck" into the search box.

3) Click the "Surf" button to see a list of websites.

With factsurfer.com, finding more information is just a click away.